W9-BAC-754

11/16—20
1/07 7
4/01
2

DEMCO

MYSTERY
OF THE
LASCAUX CAVE

MYSTERY OF THE LASCAUX CAVE

by

Dorothy Hinshaw Patent

BENCHMARK BOOKS

MARSHALL CAVENDISH
NEW YORK

With thanks to Dr. Jane Day,
former chief curator of the Denver Museum of Natural History,
who has led numerous tours of Lascaux and
whose suggestions for this book have been much appreciated.

Benchmark Books
Marshall Cavendish Corporation
99 White Plains Road
Tarrytown, New York 10591-9001

© Marshall Cavendish Corporation 1999

Library of Congress Cataloging-in-Publication Data
Patent, Dorothy Hinshaw.
Mystery of the Lascaux Cave / Dorothy Hinshaw Patent.
p.   cm. — (Frozen in time)
Includes bibliographical references and index.
Summary: Discusses the paintings on the walls of Lascaux Cave in France
including the cave's discovery, its significance, and the efforts to preserve
the paintings themselves.
ISBN 0-7614-0784-7
1. Lascaux Cave (France)—Juvenile literature. 2. Magdalenian culture—France—Montignac—Juvenile literature. 3. Cave paintings—France—Montignac—Juvenile literature. 4. Art, Prehistoric—France—Montignac—Juvenile literature. 5. Montignac (France)—Antiquities—Juvenile literature. [1. Lascaux Cave (France) 2. Magdalenian culture. 3. Cave paintings. 4. Art, Prehistoric.]
I. Title II. Series: Patent, Dorothy Hinshaw. Frozen in time.
GN772.3.M3P37   1999   936.4—dc21   97-48276   CIP   AC

Printed in Hong Kong

3 5 6 4 2

Photo research by Linda Sykes, Hilton Head, SC
Book design by Carol Matsuyama

Photo Credits
Cover: courtesy of Jean Vertut; pages 2–3, 7, 16–17, 42–43: Sisse Brimberg © National Geographic Society Image Collection; page 8: Colorphoto Hinz, Basel; page 10–11: D. Mazonowiecz © Bruce Coleman Inc., NY; page 12: Norbert Aujoulat/National Geographic Society Image Collection; page 14–15: © A. Bordes/Explorer; page 19: Jean Vertut; pages 20, 35 (bottom), 55–56: © Fanny Broadcast, Gamma Liaison; pages 22–23, 26–27: Westfalisches Schulmuseum, A K G; pages 30–31, 36–37: Bridgeman Art Library International Ltd.; page 32-33, 48: Jack Unruh © National Geographic Society Image Collection; page 35 (top): Lloyd K. Townsend © National Geographic Society Image Collection; page 38–39: © Raphael Gaillarde, Gamma Liaison ; pages 40–41, 50–51: © 1959 Rene Burri, Magnum Photos Inc.; page 45: Thomas Stephan, Ulmer Museum; page 52–53: Alexander Marshak © National Geographic Society Image Collection

Contents

Introduction

Ever since I first learned of the ancient paintings of the Lascaux cave in France, I have wanted to visit them. Created as long as 17,000 years ago, these images of now extinct wild cattle, wild horses, and other animals fascinated the world. So when I decided to write this book, I was disappointed to learn that the original Lascaux cave was closed to the public. Dr. Jane Day, of the Denver Museum of Natural History, however, told me that a few people were allowed to view the cave for research purposes. I applied for a permit and hoped.

A few weeks later, a letter in French arrived. If I appeared at Lascaux at 4:00 P.M. on October 22, 1996, it said, I would be allowed into the cave. I was thrilled!

As my husband and I drove to Lascaux, the peacefulness of the site surrounded by a lovely woodland calmed me. First we took a guided tour of Lascaux II, an amazing modern replica of the main parts of the cave that is open to the public. Then it was time for the real thing. We walked up to the locked entrance gate, where three Swedish journalists were also waiting.

The man in charge of the cave, called the curator, took us into a meeting room to talk with us. He showed us bits of ochre, one of the pigments used by the ancient artists, and let us draw with it on rocks, as they had done. He described the methods used to monitor the condition of the cave to preserve its environment. If we had any questions, we should ask them now, he said, as we'd have only thirty-five minutes in the cave, and he wanted to show us whatever he could during that short time. One of the Swedes had visited ten years before, and the curator asked him what he remembered. The Swede thought for a moment, then answered, "The impression." The curator nodded in understanding, and the rest of us wondered what he meant.

We left the room and descended the concrete steps leading to the heavy metal doors that guard the cave. We entered through a series of

France's Dordogne River Valley, where the Lascaux cave is located, has been home to humans for thousands of years.

doors, like air locks on a spaceship. Each time, the curator urged us to move quickly, to help keep out the outside air. We dipped the bottoms of our shoes in a disinfectant solution to keep out unwanted pollen, algae, bacteria, and fungi. The air inside the earth felt cool on my skin. Finally, we climbed down into the darkness on a steep metal staircase, a faint flashlight showing the way, into the ancient cave itself. A peaceful stillness surrounded us.

Lighting the way with his flashlight, the curator took us through the dark cave into a side branch called the Nave, which is not reproduced in Lascaux II. He used his flashlight to illuminate a beautiful horse pierced by a row of parallel arrowlike lines etched into the stone and showed us the mysterious signs and symbols that also marked the walls. Farther along the passageway, he aimed his light at a good-sized dark horse. Looking closely, I saw that the etched lines actually depicted at least three animals, a horse within a horse within a horse. The paint had partly flaked off from many of the paintings, but the engraved outlines still gave them a feeling of power and life. After lighting up a frieze of stag heads on the opposite wall, the curator pointed out the entrance to the shaft, a deep hole with a mystifying group of images hidden in the darkness. No one was allowed to enter there.

Next he led us into the Axial Gallery. He turned on the dim lighting, and the cave came alive with vibrant paintings of horses and wild cattle, deer and ibex (wild goats). We saw the sweep of images, all the way through the gallery to the other end, the famous Hall of the Bulls. One of the Swedes whispered excitedly, "It's all one whole, can't you see? It's all the work of one artist, I know it! Just look!" He was sure that this was the gallery of an ancient genius. I could see why he felt that way—the sense of unity was overwhelming. There were animals everywhere, brightly painted and alive, as if joyously created only yesterday.

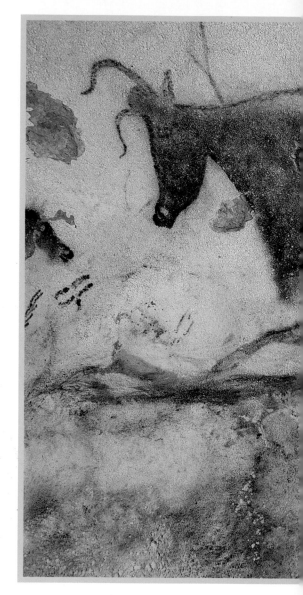

Thirty-five minutes pass very quickly when time is precious. The curator had to stick to the highlights, pointing out the similarities and differences among the famous huge bulls on the walls and ceiling. The last bull looked unfinished to me, and I asked if the people might have abandoned the cave before it was completed. The guide smiled and shook his head. "Look, the artists didn't need to paint the rest," he said. "It's there in the rock, where the paint ends." I looked closely and saw that, indeed, the rock took over, outlining the rest of the bull. The animals and the walls of the cave were one. Too soon we had to leave. It felt strange, stepping out once again into the gently filtered afternoon sunlight of the woods into a world thousands of years in the future.

Having been lucky enough to see the original cave, I now know

The walls of the Axial Gallery are covered by lively images of wild animals as well as rows of dots and other strange symbols.

what the Swede who had visited before meant about remembering the impression. At home, I study photos of particular images from the cave and don't remember seeing them. But I do remember how it felt to be in that amazing place, surrounded by such glorious evidence that human creativity is an ancient gift, not just a product of modern civilization.

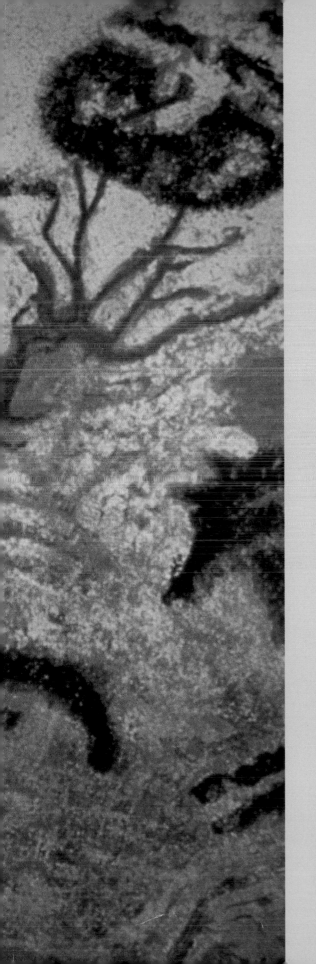

1

DISCOVERY

On September 12, 1940, four French teenagers made a discovery that would change forever the way modern humans view their prehistoric ancestors. A few days earlier, one of the boys had noticed a deep hole in the ground between the roots of a tree. Legend spoke of a secret underground passageway leading to the old manor house of Lascaux that might hold a treasure. The boy told his buddies about his discovery, and on the twelfth, they headed for the mysterious hole, armed with a knife, a homemade oil lamp, and some pieces of rope.

◄ *Deer from the walls of the Lascaux cave, with the head of a horse just showing on the right*

Jacques Marsal, one of the boys who discovered the cave, became its main guide after he grew up.

After clearing away enough stones and undergrowth to enlarge the entrance, the boys squeezed through the hole and slid down, down, down into the cave below, one by one. At first, they saw strange markings on the walls—red spots and black ones, and lines of color. Then they hung up the lamp and looked more closely. There, staring out from the walls, were images of deer, horses, and enormous bulls. The amazed boys pledged secrecy to one another—this was to be their special place. The next day, they returned and explored further, finding more and more incredible works of art.

They could not keep this find a secret—it was too exciting and wonderful— so they confided in their schoolteacher, Monsieur Laval. They widened the entrance, and the teacher joined their explorations. Later on, trying to explain his feelings, Monsieur Laval said, "I had literally gone mad."

The walls of the cave were covered with beautiful paintings. The deep, rich colors looked as if they had been applied only days before, but Monsieur Laval knew the art was ancient. He realized the potential importance of such a find. Soon the most famous prehistorian of the time, the Abbé Henri Breuil, was contacted.

Meanwhile, word got out to the public, and the nearby village of Montignac advertised the cave, only 1.2 miles (2 kilometers) away. People flocked to see the amazing art. But soon, concerns of war became more important than art. France at the time was occupied by the German army, and the French people had to focus their attention on survival. The cave was almost forgotten. After the war, a new entrance with wide metal doors was built, and a staircase was constructed leading down into the main chamber. Electricity was installed to provide light. On Bastille Day, July 14, 1948, France's most important national holiday, the public was welcomed once more.

2
THE FIND

The limestone hills of south-western France are riddled with caves. Over hundreds of thousands of years, humans have sought shelter in the mouths of these caverns, sometimes venturing deep within and leaving their mark. Before the discovery of the Lascaux cave, other caves with prehistoric art were known, but none came anywhere near the spectacular beauty and abundance of Lascaux.

Caves dot the cliffs of southwestern France. Nearby, some people still make their homes. ➤

The Hall of the Bulls

The Lascaux cave contains seven different areas with painted or engraved images. The most impressive is called the Hall of the Bulls. This is the largest part of the cave and the one into which the boys slid on that day in 1940. The walls and ceiling of the Hall of the Bulls are covered with colorful images of horses and wild cattle, painted as though

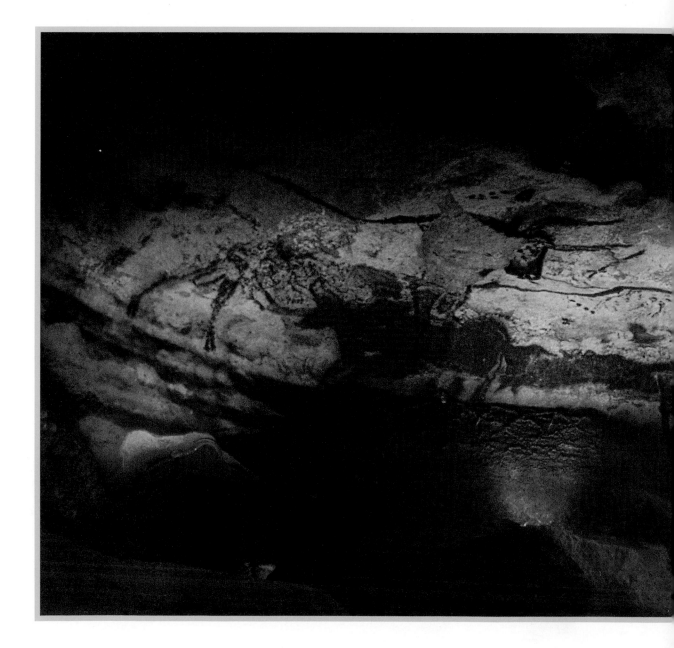

caught in movement. Four giant bulls, one almost 18 feet (5.5 meters) long, dominate the scene. Beautiful black, red, and yellow horses prance among the bulls, along with a few small but magnificently horned stags. On one wall, the somewhat deteriorated image of a bear

The Hall of the Bulls leading into the Axial Gallery. You can see the head of one giant bull on the left, as well as the other three bulls.

blends into the belly of one of the giant bulls. All these images are very lifelike. But just to the left of the entrance, a mythical creature with two long, slender horns and a row of strange oval markings along its body graces the wall. This image is the only one that does not represent a real animal. Even though it has two horns, it is often referred to as the unicorn. (See the title page of this book for a picture of the unicorn.)

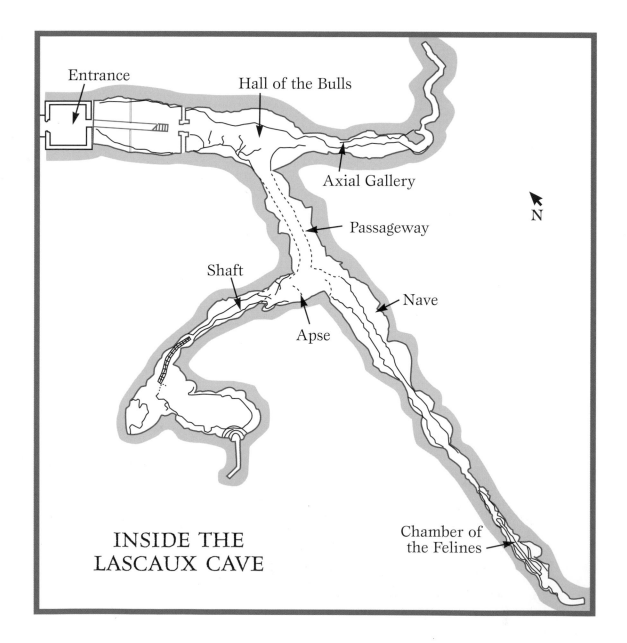

INSIDE THE
LASCAUX CAVE

The walls of the Axial Gallery are covered with images, mostly of horses, but also of cattle, such as the one here, which seems to be jumping over the horses.

Exploring the Cave

Straight ahead of the Hall of the Bulls, in the Axial Gallery, horses dominate, along with a number of cattle. One cow appears to be leaping over a row of small, dark ponies. At the far end, the Axial Gallery narrows into a descending tunnel too small to enter. Just in front of the tunnel, high along the left wall, a series of horses gallop, the last one upside down above the dark tunnel entrance, as if it had run over a cliff and fallen.

To the right of the Hall of the Bulls is the Passageway, which leads into the Nave. Its walls are covered with the images of horses and other animals, including some bison. During the thousands of years that the cave was closed off, small currents of air through the Nave brushed against the walls, flaking off pigment from many of the

How Limestone Caves Form

Limestone, also called calcium carbonate, is soft and dissolves easily in water. Through the ages, underground springs and streams work their way through it, dissolving and washing away sections of the limestone, creating caves and passageways. Once caves are formed, they continue to change as water filters through the overlying soil, dissolving more limestone. But when this water encounters the air in caves, it releases some of the calcium carbonate it carries. The calcium carbonate precipitates out, forming new rock called calcite. Calcite from dripping water forms stalactites, which hang from cave ceilings, and stalagmites, which grow from the floors. Calcite can also line cave walls, hardening them, and cover cave floors, preserving in stone any items that humans or animals may have left there thousands of years ago.

Cosquer cave, one of the many caves in southwestern France. Its stalactites and stalagmites form an eerie landscape.

paintings. Fortunately, the engraving remains, so the outlines are still clear. High on one wall, sheltered from the air currents, a line of five stags appear on a naturally dark part of the wall. They seem to be holding their heads just above the water as they swim across a river.

On one side of the Nave, beyond the area called the Apse, is the Shaft, about 16 feet (5 meters) below the level of the rest of the cave. There, in the darkness, a few strange sketchlike images appear on the walls: the only rhinoceros in the cave, a bison that appears to have been injured by a spear, a stick figure of a human with a bird's head, and a stick with a simple bird image on top.

Like the Axial Gallery, the Nave narrows at its far end. But farther along, the funnel widens slightly, and there are more engraved images in the area called the Chamber of the Felines. Horses and bison share the walls with what seem to be lions.

Signs and Symbols

Throughout the cave, amid the lifelike animal images, are about four hundred signs and symbols. Some of these are sticklike, either single or in parallel sets. Others are branchlike, while still others have curved lines. Some of the lines look like arrows. Rows of large red or black dots mark the walls in many places. Perhaps the most puzzling markings are squares, most of which are subdivided into smaller squares. The smaller squares may be painted in different colors or left blank. The feet of the animals sometimes touch or penetrate the squares.

3

THE PEOPLE OF LASCAUX

The cave of Lascaux gives us the gift of beautiful art. In addition to the art, the cave has yielded lamps for burning animal fat, fragments of rope, engraving tools, and other bits and pieces that offer hints of how the walls were painted. But still, we know little about the lives and times of the people who created these great images.

One artist's impression of how early hunters might have lived ▶

Most archaeologists agree on the time span during which prehistoric people visited the cave, even though the pigments in the paints the artists used were made from minerals and cannot be dated. (Only materials that were once alive can be dated, by measuring the amount of carbon-14 they contain.) Fortunately, fossilized pollen, bones, and charcoal remains tell us the cave was in use starting about 17,000 years ago and was last visited, before 1940, about 8,000 years ago.

Ancient Humans in Europe

Southwestern France has been inhabited by humans for at least 400,000 years. The area provided a relatively mild climate much of the time, good hunting, ground rich in flint for making tools, and many caves. People didn't normally live deep inside the caves, but cave entrances provided natural shelters from the weather.

Many different cultures developed and died out over the tens of thousands of years that our species, *Homo sapiens,* inhabited the area. The people who lived in southwestern France during the years the Lascaux cave was decorated are called the Magdalenians by archaeologists. The name comes from a rock shelter called La Madeleine on the shore of the Vezere River, discovered in 1863. It yielded a number of important finds, including the skeleton of a child, prehistoric implements, and works of art. The Magdalenian period ran from around 15,000 to 9000 B.C. and was characterized by fine works of art. The most impressive works that have survived to modern times are the images of Lascaux.

The Magdalenians had well-developed flint tools, as well as ivory and bone weapons such as harpoons, and javelins made from reindeer antlers. They probably also made tools and weapons from wood, bark, and leather, but these items would have disappeared over the thousands of passing years.

The Magdalenians were hunters, mainly of reindeer. Most of the bones found on the floor of the Lascaux cave, which represent the remains of what people ate while in the cave, are from reindeer. At

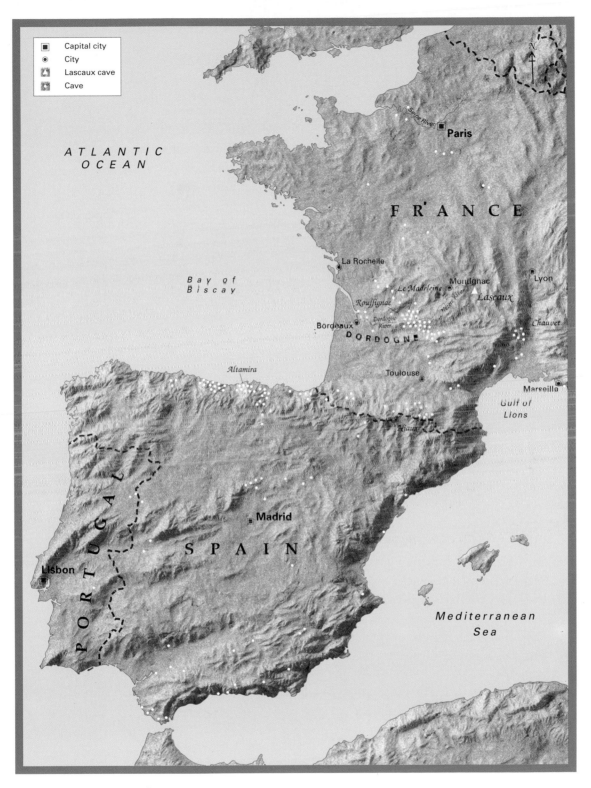

Legend
- ■ Capital city
- ◉ City
- ◮ Lascaux cave
- ▣ Cave

ATLANTIC
OCEAN

Seine River
■ **Paris**

F R A N C E

La Rochelle
Montignac ◉ Lyon
Le Madeleine
Rouffignac ◮ *Lascaux*
Vezere River
Dordogne River *Chauvet*
Bordeaux
D O R D O G N E

Bay of Biscay

Altamira
Toulouse
Marseille

Niaux
Gulf of Lions

P O R T U G A L

S P A I N
■ **Madrid**

Mediterranean Sea

Lisbon ■

THE CAVES OF FRANCE AND SPAIN

Early Humans in Europe

T he first humans evolved in Africa and moved from there to other parts of the world. Archaeologists working in the 1990s have pushed the arrival of humans in Europe back hundreds of thousands of years. Some 800,000-year-old fossils found in a Spanish cave indicate that the first humans may have arrived in Europe more than a million years ago.

Scientists haven't agreed about what species these early arrivals represent, but many believe the best candidate is called *Homo erectus.* This species evolved in Africa about two million years ago. Like us, it walked on two legs, but its body was more powerfully built. Its forehead sloped backward, and it had a bony ridge above the eyes. Over time, this species evolved into more advanced kinds of humans.

One of these, a species that lived in the Middle East, Europe, and central Asia starting about 230,000 years ago, is the Neanderthal. Scientists call it *Homo neanderthalensis.* Neanderthals disappeared around 30,000 years ago. No one can say for sure why, but many scientists believe that in some way, the arrival of our species in the Middle East and Europe resulted in the extinction of the Neanderthals.

The Neanderthals were shorter and more powerfully built than our ancestors, but in some ways they were similar. Neanderthals made stone tools and buried their dead. Recently, a bone flute was found in a cave inhabited by Neanderthals, suggesting that they enjoyed music. No art created by Neanderthals has been discovered yet, however.

Fossils of our direct ancestors, the first *Homo sapiens,* have been found in Africa and Asia, dating from 400,000 to 100,000 years ago. Over time, *Homo sapiens* changed and evolved until their fossil skulls and other bones came to look like ours today. Scientists call these modern humans *Homo sapiens sapiens,* to distinguish them from earlier types. *Homo sapiens sapiens* seems to have arrived in Europe about 40,000 years ago. The name Cro-Magnon is used for these people in Ice Age Europe. While Cro-Magnons were like us, their skeletons were more sturdy. It is the Cro-Magnons who created Ice Age art. Around 10,000 years ago, toward the end of the Ice Age cold, the bones of *Homo sapiens sapiens* began to become lighter, more like the skeletons of humans today.

Note: The information above is up-to-date as of the writing of this book. Archaeologists keep finding more human fossils and tools. These finds often require changes in our thinking about early humans. For example, scientists once thought Neanderthals belonged in the species *Homo sapiens.* But now we know that these ancient humans were different enough to be placed in their own species.

Early people used the mouths of caves for shelter, but didn't actually live deep within them.

that time, no humans had yet begun to domesticate animals (except perhaps wolves) or plant crops, so people the world over depended on hunting and the gathering of food for survival.

Ice Ages and Animals

During Ice Age times, many large animals shared the land with the people—reindeer, bison, deer, mammoths, wild horses, wild cattle, rhinoceroses, lions, and bears. The types of animals found in southern France varied, depending on the climate, which changed as the sheets of ice crept down from the north and receded again. During the coldest times, reindeer were the most abundant animals. When the climate warmed up and the edges of the glaciers receded, the reindeer moved north and animals from farther south, such as deer, horses, and cattle, replaced them.

Some of these animals are still with us in different form, and others have disappeared. Wild horses lived in the area over a period of thousands of years, through cold and mild periods. The horses of the time probably came in a number of varieties, each adapted to somewhat different climatic conditions. The aurochs were the ancestors of our domesticated cattle. A giant beast, the aurochs had a body up to 10 feet (3 meters) long and a 6-foot-tall (1.8-meter-tall) shoulder. The ibex, a wild goat, is also illustrated at Lascaux. At the time, ibex were common and lived in the hills. Today, they are endangered and inhabit only protected parks and high, rocky mountains.

Life in Magdalenian Times

The Magdalenians sometimes built their shelters in cave mouths, using the natural overhang to help protect their home. They made clothing from animal skins sewn using bone or antler needles. The paintings show us that there was much more to the lives of the people than mere survival. They had a highly developed artistic sense, and something about their culture led them to work hard to perfect their

The Ice Age in Europe

T hrough the time of the dinosaurs, the earth's climate was generally warm and humid. Palm trees grew in what is now Canada, and similar forms of life thrived everywhere.

Then, around 67 million years ago, things began to change. Although there are many theories as to what made things different, no one can be sure. But change did come. Temperatures began to drop, and ice sheets formed at the South Pole. As the climate became even cooler, ice formed in the north as well.

The most recent cycle of ice ages began about 3.25 million years ago. Glaciers in Europe, northern Asia, and North America advanced and retreated, changing the climate from cold to mild and back again over and over. The last Ice Age in this cycle of four began around 110,000 years ago, with its height occurring between about 25,000 and 15,000 years ago. Temperatures around the world reached their lowest levels, and the ice spread farthest south. So much water was locked up in ice that sea levels were much lower than today. Scientists believe that most of the migration of people from Asia into North America occurred during this time, when a land bridge existed between the continents where the Bering Sea is today.

In Europe, this period was called the Würm Glaciation. Much of northern Europe was covered with ice. The northern ice extended as far south as what is now Dresden, Germany, an area that today has a climate similar to the American Midwest. Farther south, glaciers in the Alps reached down into the valleys.

About 10,000 years ago, the climate began to warm once more, until today glaciers are limited to polar regions and mountainous areas, mostly in the north. Grasslands were taken over by forests, and the great herds of grazing animals disappeared. The hunting peoples who created magnificent cave paintings and engravings also seem to have vanished. Our species, hunters for so long, began to cultivate crops and domesticate animals. An entirely new kind of culture emerged, based on raising food rather than hunting and gathering it from nature.

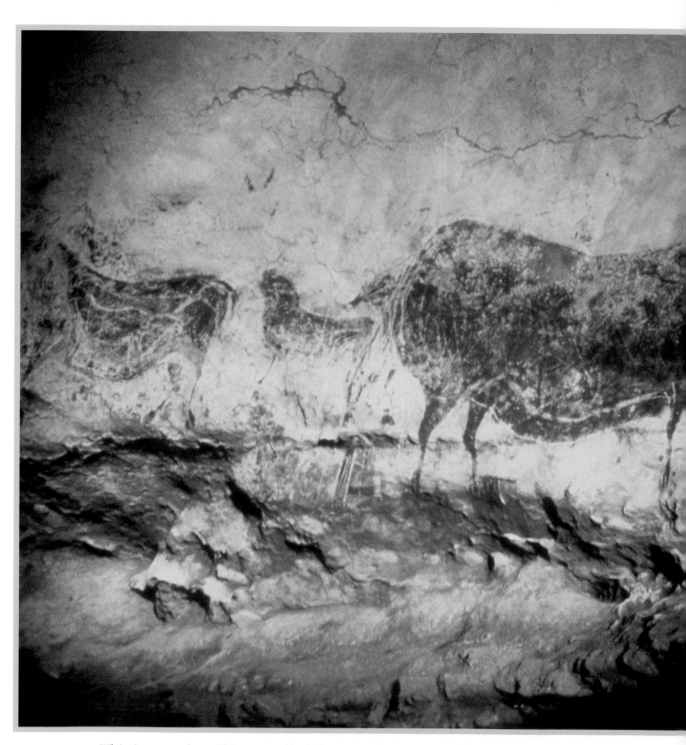

This image of a wild cow, called the aurochs, is especially beautiful. It was painted in the Nave at Lascaux.

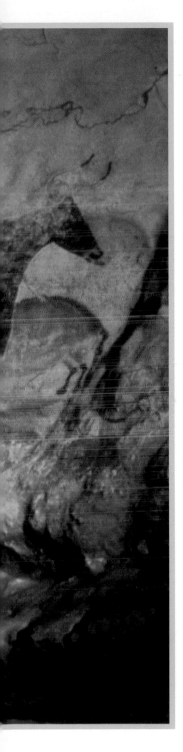

art. The art in the cave was created by practiced artists who had spent a great deal of time developing their style and their technique. The Magdalenians may have even painted brilliant images on animal skins, tree bark, or their own bodies. But since these forms of art don't survive for thousands of years, we will never know.

During the early Magdalenian period, when the Lascaux paintings were produced, the climate in the area was fairly mild, but cooler than today. Winters were snowy, but summers could be warm. It was a time when the glaciers of the Ice Age had receded somewhat to the north. When the glaciers once again moved southward, the people left the area.

About eight thousand years ago, other people visited the cave, leaving behind charcoal from their torches, which scientists have dated. What were these people like, and what did they think of the paintings they saw? The art might have been ancient and alien to them, nine thousand years old, perhaps created by a completely different culture. Sometime after these last visitors departed, the entrance to the cave collapsed, sealing it and protecting it from the outside environment for thousands of years.

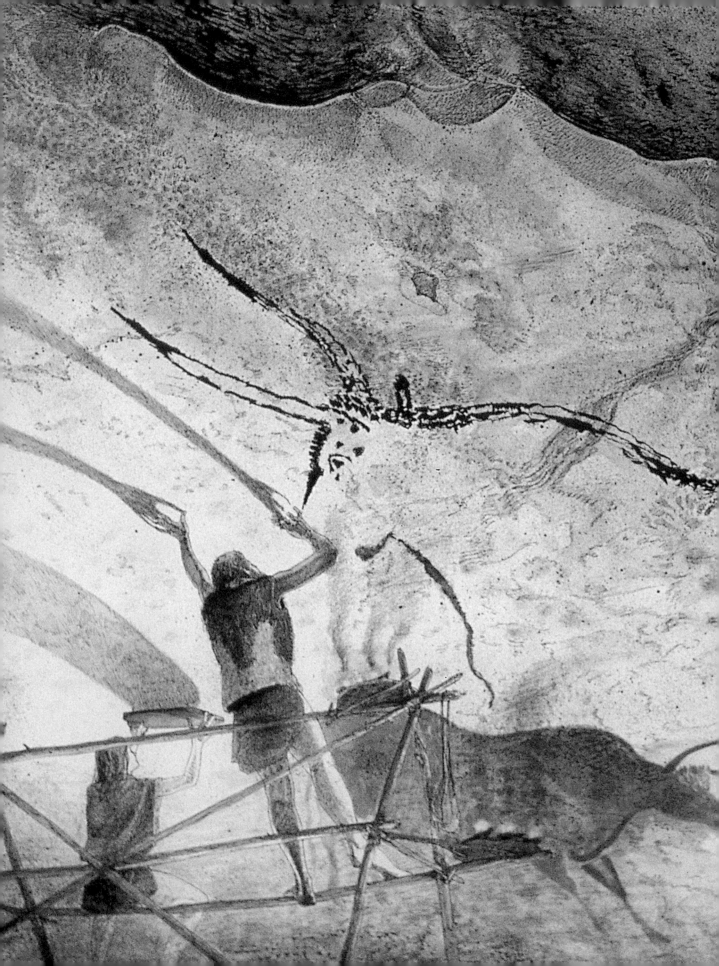

4

PAINTING THE CAVE

Try to imagine being a Lascaux cave artist. We are used to being able to sketch something we want to draw, using a pencil. If we make a mistake, we can use an eraser and start all over again. But the Lascaux artists had to get it right the first time. One of the reasons the paintings in the Hall of the Bulls and the Axial Gallery survived so beautifully is the nature of the cave walls. Ordinary limestone can be engraved with stone tools to create images like the animals in the Nave. But the limestone walls of the Hall of the Bulls and Axial Gallery had been coated by a thin layer of harder calcite deposited there by water. They were too hard to engrave. When a line

◄ *Holes in the walls and bits of wood found in the cave indicate that the Lascaux artists used scaffolding to allow them to reach the upper walls and ceiling.*

of color was drawn on these walls, the pigment fused immediately with the wall, combining with it chemically. No mistakes could be made, since erasing was impossible.

It's clear that the artists of Lascaux were not mere doodlers. They were highly experienced, and they knew exactly what they were doing when they produced their masterpieces. The society of the time must have valued their work highly, allowing them to take time to perfect their art. While most people were occupied in basic activities such as hunting for meat, gathering plant foods, making clothing, and so forth, these great artists were practicing. Perhaps they developed their talent and technique on the outside cliff walls. Archaeologists have found traces of painting materials along the bases of some of the cliffs.

Painting Techniques

The Lascaux paintings were all done in earth colors, using pigments found in rocks. Ochre and hematite are iron compounds that come in shades of yellow, red, and brown. Black and dark brown were painted with manganese compounds. A violet color also came from a manganese mineral. No greens or blues are present, and chances are they were never used, although they could have been there once and faded with time.

Some of the pigments occur as soft stones that could have been used to draw directly on the rock. But most of the work was done with paint. To make the paint, the artists pounded the minerals into powder, then mixed the powder with water to form a paste. Getting the right color was important. There is evidence that the artists mixed pigments to get the desired shade and sometimes heated them to create subtle color variations.

We can't be sure what the artists used for brushes, but bits of fur, moss, or human hair could have held the paint without dripping. The bodies of many of the animals were painted by dabbing circles of paint close together, creating a dappled effect. Hollow bone tubes were also used to blow large areas of powdered paint onto the damp

Ice Age caves often have ancient images of human hands, produced when the artist pressed a hand against the wall, then blew powdered paint to fill in the outline.

walls. Such tubes were found by archaeologists in the thin layer of calcite formed over thousands of years on the floor of the cave. Tools and scrapers, worn down from engraving the walls, were also found on the cave floor.

Much of the art at Lascaux is high on the walls and on the ceiling. Archaeologists found holes that held the ends of wooden scaffolds, along with the clay used to anchor them. They also found bits of a rope made from braided plant fibers. Such rope could have been used to lash the scaffolding together. Small fat-burning lamps provided dim, flickering light, and the bits of charcoal found on the cave floor indicate that torches could have lit the cave as well.

Experts at Work

The experience of the artists shows up in many ways. Some of the large bulls are painted over an uneven area so that the artist couldn't see one end of the bull while painting the other. Even so, the proportions are correct. The artists created a sense of depth by leaving a gap between the body and the limbs on the far side, which tricks the eye into seeing three dimensions.

Over and over again, the artists also used the contours of the cave in their work. In the Hall of the Bulls, the ledges along the sides are used to represent the ground on which many of the animals are running. Some animals are drawn to take advantage of bumps in the cave wall. In one place, a hollow in the cave wall represents a pregnant cow's belly. In another, a bit of rock represents the eye of a horse. Unfortunately, this use of the rock contours to create a three-dimensional effect can't be seen well in photographs.

The style used in many of the paintings shows the body from the side but the head as if turned and the hooves from the front view, all

The Lascaux artist who painted these bison created a sense of depth by making one animal seem to be in front of the other.

on the same animal. This was called "twisted perspective" by the Abbé Breuil, who thought of it as a primitive trait. Nowadays, twisted perspective, along with the often short legs and swollen bellies of some of the animals, is considered a matter of the style of painting, rather than an early stage in the development of art.

Ice Age Art in Europe

The first Ice Age art was found by archaeologists in the early 1800s. The two harpoons decorated with geometric designs and the reindeer bone engraved with two deer, found in Switzerland and France, created quite a stir. By the 1860s, a number of decorated objects had been dug up in caves. Since they were found with stone tools and the bones of long-extinct animals, no one doubted they were very old. But when the daughter of an archaeologist exploring the Spanish cave of Altamira in 1879 looked up at the ceiling and saw a parade of animals painted there, no one believed that what she had found was ancient. It wasn't until early in the twentieth century that paintings on cave walls were accepted as examples of prehistoric art.

Much of the Ice Age art discovered in Europe consists of paintings and engravings on rocks. Engravings, which might have once been painted, are found in a number of rock shelters as well as caves. Altogether, there are about 150 sites featuring Ice Age paintings and engravings.

Archaeologists and art historians have struggled for decades to arrange the many finds into some ordered system. Unfortunately, many of the small items that could be carried were collected without much information, and many of the cave paintings were made using pigments that can't be dated. Even so, attempts have been made to make sense of this wonderful puzzle.

Until 1994 some experts on European prehistoric art believed they could see an evolving improvement in cave art over thousands of years, with Lascaux being the high point, the example showing final mastery of artistic expression. The age of the oldest items in the cave—17,000 years old—was taken as the earliest possible date for refined art.

Then in December 1994, three French explorers made an amazing discovery. They found a cave whose walls were covered with powerful images of ancient animals, not only the horses, cattle, and so forth found in Lascaux, but also lions and bears. Fortunately, two of the discoverers were archaeologists, and all three were dedicated to studying the find carefully and scientifically.

Some of the beautiful drawings in the cave were made with charcoal, so dating them was possible. With modern techniques, even a tiny sample can give a date accurate to within a few hundred years. Three samples were dated. The results were totally surprising: all three drawings were at least 30,000 years old!

This cave, called Chauvet after one of its discoverers, has changed the way archaeologists and art historians view the creative aspect of human culture. The Chauvet art is not at all "primitive." Clearly, the ability to produce great art did not slowly evolve toward the high point of Lascaux. A new way must be found to think about the origins of creativity.

New dating techniques allow charcoal used in Ice Age art to be dated. One animal in this painting from the Niaux cave dates from about 13,850 years ago. Another was created almost a thousand years later, around 12,890 years ago.

5

THE MYSTERY OF LASCAUX

We can never know for sure just why the Lascaux cave, or any other cave, was painted. Over time, people have come up with a number of theories, and the debate continues to this day.

How can we approach this question? We don't even know the exact time span over which the paintings were made. We

No matter what theories people come up with to explain why ancient artists painted Lascaux, we will never know the answer for certain. ➤

don't know whether these images followed one another by days, months, years, decades, or millennia. We also don't know if all the paintings and engravings were made for the same reason. The strange drawings in the Shaft are separated in subject matter, space, and style from the rest of the cave, as is the art in the isolated Chamber of the Felines. And the main cave areas themselves show horses painted in more than one style. And then there are the mysterious signs and symbols.

Some archaeologists today think the images helped store information about the natural world, such as the behavior of animals. Perhaps they somehow functioned as a model of the specific landscape near the caves. Maybe they helped illustrate myths and stories important to the clan or tribe.

Helping the Hunt

The art found in prehistoric European caves was once thought to represent "hunting magic." Archaeologists believed that the artists painted horses and bulls in hopes of improving their luck in the hunt. Perhaps the animal images were in movement because they were in flight from hunters. Some of the lines on the walls may represent arrows aimed at the fleeing animals. The strange square symbols may be traps holding the animals' feet. The jumping cow was thought not to be jumping over the horses but rather trying to skid to a stop to avoid being caught

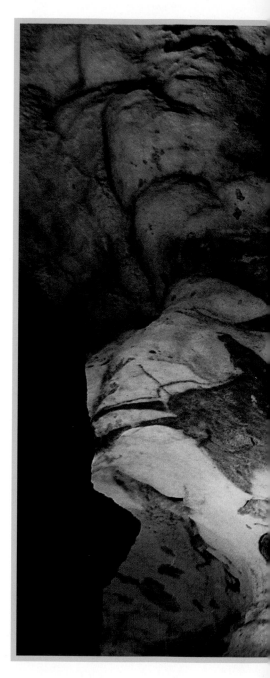

in the "trap" in front of it. According to this theory, the animals pierced by arrowlike lines represent an attempt to magically bring successful hunting, and the upside-down horse has been driven over a cliff by successful hunters.

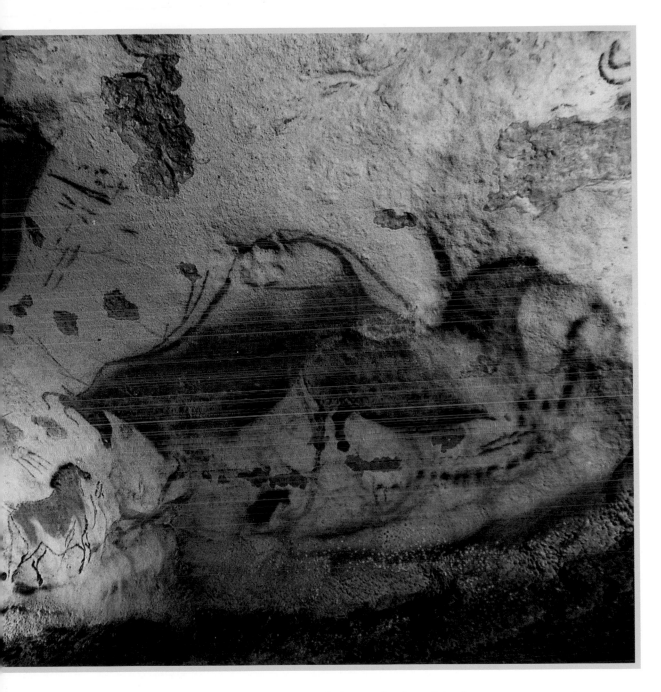

Many mysterious signs and symbols can be found in the Lascaux cave paintings. Notice the row of black dots underneath the horse on the right, the four red lines with two squares on top just above the second horse on the left, the black dashed lines in front of that same horse's muzzle, and the feathery symbol on that horse's belly. Look closely at the picture, and you'll find still more markings.

Artists and Society

For art to flourish, a society must be able to release some of its members from the duty of obtaining food. But when people today think about prehistoric hunter-gatherers, they usually imagine a struggle for survival in a hostile world. Wouldn't the search for food have been constant and the possibility of starvation always present? Actually, we know little about how difficult it might have been to get food in those days. It could have been relatively easy, if herds of reindeer and horses were abundant.

Chances are that during the period when the Lascaux art was produced, finding enough to eat wasn't all that hard. We don't know if the artists who created these great paintings and engravings were men, women, or both. But the artists must have been allowed to develop their talents over a period of years. They needed time to master the techniques of grinding and blending pigments and of doing the actual painting and engraving.

Even though life was very different then than now, the people of southwestern France in prehistoric times were like us. The differences were in their way of life, not their biology. The urge to produce art seems to be a universal human trait. Rock art in Europe has survived for at least 30,000 years, and there is no reason to think people only became artists at that time. They could have been drawing and painting on animal skins or pieces of wood that have not survived, or their efforts might remain to be discovered.

Not only must it be possible for some members to be free of the obligation to find food, society itself must have a strong reason for releasing artists from ordinary duties so they can explore their talents. Clearly, the societies that produced rock art around the world many thousands of years ago believed that art was important. The artists must have known that they would be supported by the other members of the society, that someone would make sure they were fed, clothed, and housed.

We don't know the motives of society so long ago in allowing artists the time to devote themselves to their art. But artists then probably felt much as artists do today. From the artists' point of view, the important thing is always to express their talent and their feelings through their art. Artists are not primarily concerned with society's "reason" for supporting their work. The challenge and the joy of the work itself is what matters. We can feel fortunate that these artists were allowed to create and that their masterpieces were preserved through time for our appreciation and enjoyment.

This statuette has survived about 30,000 years. It was found in Germany and shows a human with a feline head.

Today, most archaeologists have dismissed the hunting magic theory, partly because we now know these people focused much of their hunting on reindeer, yet there are no images of reindeer in the cave. If the artists were trying to improve the hunt, one would expect their most usual prey to be prominently featured in their art.

Initiation into the Tribe

Most cultures around the world pinpoint a time in a boy's life when he becomes a man. Jewish tradition, for example, marks this passage into manhood with the Bar Mitzvah celebration when a boy turns thirteen. In some African tribes, the adult men kidnap the older boys and take them into the forest for a period of days or even weeks. The boys must go through tests of their courage and strength, and they learn secrets of manhood. When they return to the village, they are no longer boys but men.

We know that the people who painted the Lascaux cave were hunters. Farming wasn't developed until thousands of years later, so people had to depend on nature to provide their food. Hunting tribes in some parts of the world still identify themselves with certain animals, called totems. The details differ, but the basic idea is a special association of the tribe with that animal and with its traits.

The Lascaux cave could have been the site for initiation of young people into the tribe. This may have happened over a span of time that involved more than one tribe or clan, each with its own totem animal. Perhaps a tribe with the horse for its totem animal came first. When the time arrived for boys to become young men, or girls to become women, they could have been led into the dark cave. Torches with flickering flames could have been swept across the walls, making the rows of horses appear to be running. Recently, experiments in decorated caves have shown that sound echoes in painted areas but not in unpainted parts. In such a cave, a person could clap his hands near the horse images, making a sound like a herd galloping.

Other tribes might have followed—maybe a tribe with cattle for a totem, then ones with bison, deer, ibex. This idea helps explain why only these species are present in any number in the cave, while other animals hunted at the time, such as mammoths and reindeer, are completely absent. Another idea is that the cave could have been a gathering place for various clans with different totem animals. Another cave (Rouffignac), decorated thousands of years later, features a large number of mammoths. Perhaps it was used by a tribe with the mammoth for a totem.

Shamanism

In recent years, interest in rock art around the world has increased. Archaeologists are trying to see if they can find common threads in ancient art from Australia, Africa, Europe, and North America. One strong possibility that could apply to at least some of the Ice Age art in Europe is that the art was related to religious or healing rituals.

Many cultures rely on special members of the tribe, called shamans. These people are thought to have unique powers that allow them to communicate with the spirit world. Drugs and rhythmic music help the shaman go into a deep trance. The belief is that while the shaman is in the trance, his or her soul leaves the physical body to visit the spirit world and to learn such important things as how to cure a sick tribal member or how to make a hunt successful.

When a shaman enters a trance, his vision is affected. Certain geometric patterns appear, such as grids or lattices, dots, or parallel lines. As the trance deepens, these shapes take on the form of objects in the shaman's mind, which begin to seem real.

Scientists such as Jean Clottes, an adviser for prehistoric art at the French Ministry of Culture, think that rock art could be related to shamanism. They believe the geometric patterns found in rock art around the world may represent the images seen by a shaman entering a trance. Clottes hopes to add to our understanding of ancient lifeways by examining French Ice Age cave art from the viewpoint of shamanism. "The shamanistic theory can't explain everything about

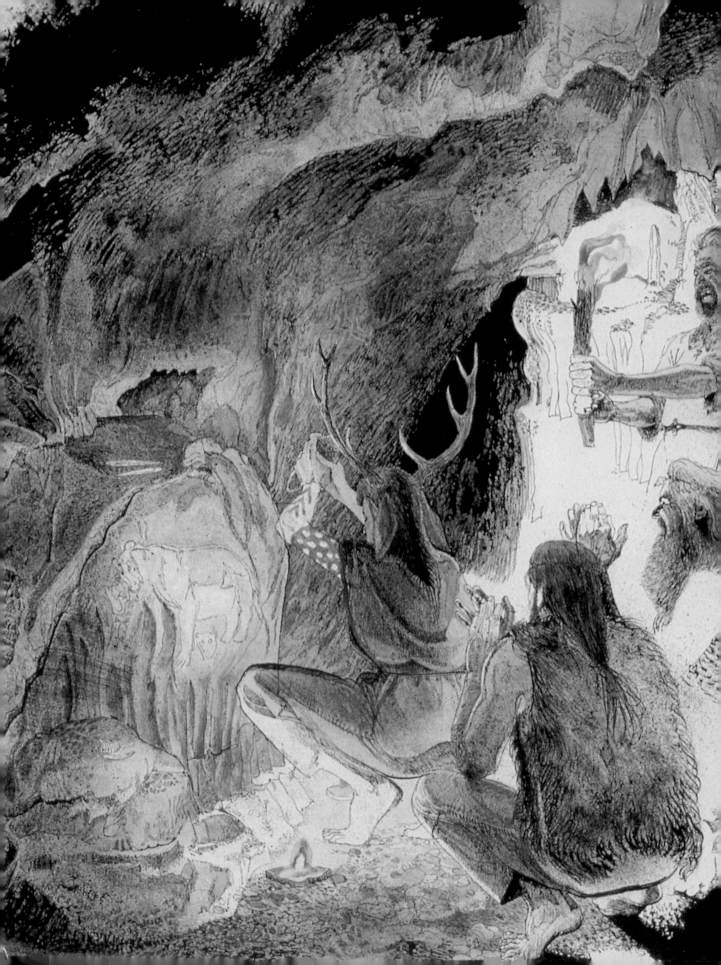

this art," he says, "but it explains more than any other theory we have right now."

The ideas of Clottes and those who work with him only deal with one way rock art may relate to shamanism. Their theories seem to help explain the geometric symbols on the walls of the Lascaux cave. But what about the animal images? Shamanism may also help to explain these. Shamans have powerful relationships with special animals that help them in their dealings with the spirit world. The Lascaux paintings and engravings may represent these animal helpers. People today, such as some Inuit, or Eskimos, who have recently lived much like Ice Age Europeans, don't feel the separation we do from the natural world. Their stories tell of humans, such as shamans, becoming animals, and animals turning into humans. Perhaps the Lascaux images can help illustrate this connection between human beings and the animal world.

Shamanism is a complex and varied aspect of spiritual life. We can only imagine what role it might have played in the lives of the people of Lascaux. Their world was so completely different from ours. They lived in close association with the great herds of animals, and they saw them very differently. Today, our domesticated animals work for us or make our lives more fun. But 17,000 years ago, people did not raise animals for food or keep them as pets. Instead, wild animals were the Magdalenians' most important food; they needed them for survival. The images of Lascaux affect us on a very deep level, one we can't understand with our minds. Perhaps they are touching something that is still a part of us, despite the separation of our lives from nature.

◄ *Shamans practice mysterious ceremonies in an ancient cave. Perhaps they're trying to make sure a hunt will be successful. This is one artist's idea of what Ice Age shamanism may have been like.*

6

SAVING LASCAUX

When Lascaux was opened to the public in 1948, it was an instant success. People from around the world flocked to see the magnificent art. During the 1950s, about six hundred people a day visited the cave. By the end of the day, visitors and guides complained of headaches when they came out. So many people in such a small space used up most of the oxygen present and breathed out large quantities of carbon dioxide. Along with the carbon dioxide came water vapor and body heat. When humid air warmed by the visitors' bodies came in contact with the cool cave wall, tiny water droplets formed. When the

◄ *From the time Lascaux was opened to the public in 1948 until it was closed in 1963, crowds of people from all over the world came to see it.*

droplets fell, they carried small bits of the paint with them.

Officials became so concerned that they installed a ventilation system in 1958. Air was sucked in from outside, filtered and cooled, controlled for humidity, and circulated into the cave. Excess carbon dioxide was removed. Now, the officials thought, even more people could be allowed into the cave without damaging it.

In 1962, as many as 1,500 visitors entered the cave each day. Tourism boomed in the area, creating many jobs. But Lascaux was getting sicker. Tour guides noticed small green spots on the cave walls. Within a few months, there were seven hundred green blotches. This was called the green disease. In addition, small white nodules appeared on the walls. This was the white disease.

Closing the Cave

In 1963, Lascaux was closed to the public. A group of scientists studied the cave and its problems like doctors examining and treating a patient. They discovered that the green disease was caused by algae and bacteria that grew because of the lights used to illuminate the cave for tourists. Careful washing of the walls with formaldehyde and antibiotics cured the green disease. But the white disease could not be removed. The nodules were small lumps of calcite that had formed because of the moisture in people's breath.

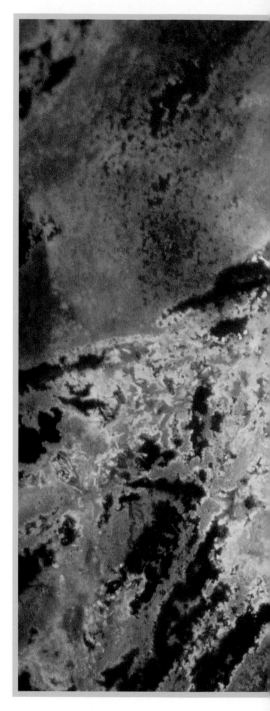

In 1965, the scientists announced that they had been able to save Lascaux. The damage from the green disease had been removed, and the white disease had not completely destroyed any of the art. But

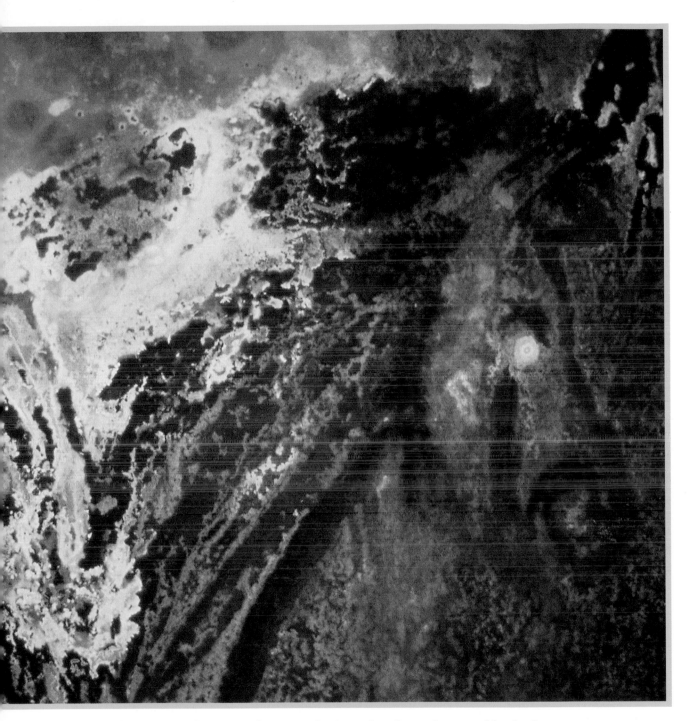

This Ice Age horse in the cave of Niaux has been damaged by both green and white disease. Algae and bacteria changed the original rich colors to eerie pastel shades. The horse's "eye," which appears to glow, is actually a spot of calcite.

from then on, the cave would have to be carefully guarded. No longer could tourists be allowed inside.

Scientists found that just one person walking in a cave for an hour releases 21 to 26 quarts (20 to 25 liters) of carbon dioxide and 1 ounce (30 grams) of water. In addition, that person releases heat the equivalent of a 175-watt lightbulb. No wonder the cave became sick. When 1,500 tourists a day visited, the water released by their bodies condensed into droplets when it touched the cool walls. Their presence was like spraying a mist of 21 quarts (20 liters) of water on the walls and floor of the cave every day. The electric lights, plus the heat released by people's bodies, raised the temperature significantly, and the carbon dioxide in their breath dissolved in the water and then became calcite, which began to form nodules as well as a film over the paintings.

Now, the temperature and humidity in the cave are measured constantly. No more than twenty people a week can enter Lascaux after obtaining special permits. They are allowed in groups of no more than five and can stay for only thirty-five minutes. Any longer would risk the future of the cave. Even in that short time, the five visitors and their guide raise the temperature inside by nearly a degree Fahrenheit.

Lascaux II

Closing Lascaux to the public was a difficult decision. People from around the world came to see the great cave, and now they had no place to go. So the French decided to create a replica of the cave that would enable people to experience the awe and wonder of the rock art without damaging the original.

It was an enormous project that took years. Three-dimensional photographs of the Hall of the Bulls and the Axial Gallery enabled workers to construct a duplicate of every lump and bump on the walls and ceiling. This was done using painstakingly molded reinforced concrete.

Once the walls were in place, artist Monique Peytral carefully copied the cave paintings, using the same materials and methods as the ancient artists. The result is a beautiful replica visited by 300,000 tourists and schoolchildren every year, as well as a museum displaying tools and lamps found in the original cave.

The ancient cave is safe, and its twin can be appreciated by people from around the world. The amazing art of Lascaux, engraved and painted thousands of years ago, provides us with a powerful connection to our ancestors.

Lascaux in Time

Europe

75,000 B.P.
Ice sheets
begin to
advance

40,000 B.P.
*Homo sapiens
sapiens*
spreads throug[h]
Europe

The World

55,000 B.P.
Human
colonization
of Australia

45,000 B.P.
World's
first known
rock art,
Australia

Note: B.P. stands for "Before Present."

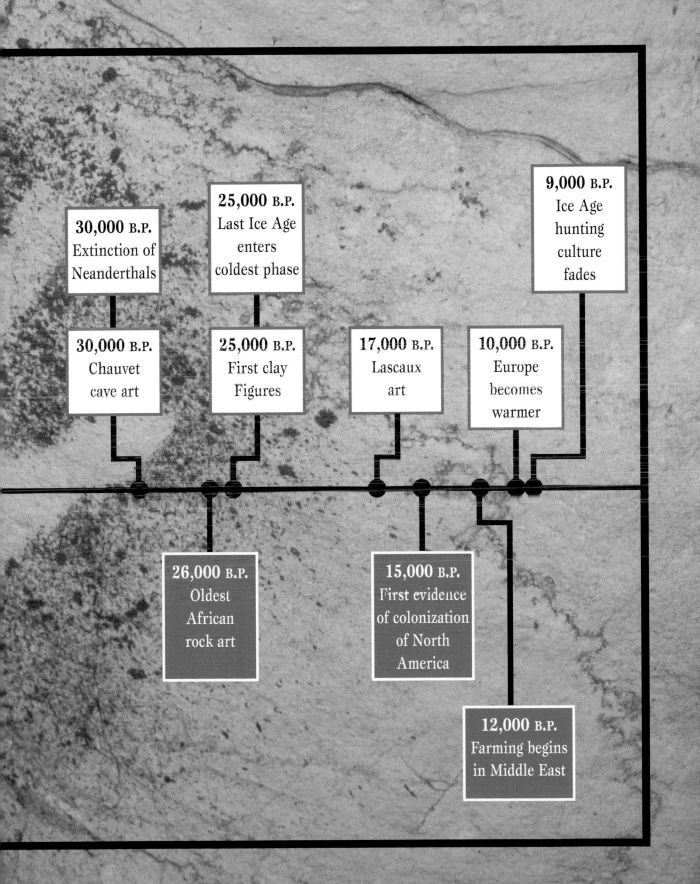

Glossary

archaeologist: A scientist who studies human history, mostly unwritten, to see how ancient peoples lived. An archaeologist digs up the remains of ancient cities and studies the tools, weapons, and pottery found.

aurochs: The wild cattle, now extinct, that were the ancestors of domesticated cattle.

calcite: A common form of calcium carbonite that makes up limestone.

clan: A division of a tribe that comes from the same ancestor.

engraving: An image carved or cut into a material such as stone.

fossils: The hardened remains of living things from the past, which have been preserved in the earth. Fossils can be bones, teeth, footprints, or other signs of life.

frieze: A series of decorative images or paintings on a wall.

glacier: A thick layer of ice, formed from snow, that flows slowly down slopes.

Homo erectus: A human species that lived from about 2 million years ago until 400,000 to 200,000 years ago.

Homo sapiens: The species that includes modern humans and those from earlier times.

Homo sapiens sapiens: The recent subspecies of humans, which includes both modern humans and Cro-Magnons.

ibex: A kind of wild goat.

ice age: A period of time when glaciers cover much of the earth's surface.

limestone: A mineral made up mainly of calcium carbonate. Limestone often is formed when water becomes saturated with minerals.

Magdalenian period: The period from about 17,000 to 11,000 years ago in Europe. The painters of Lascaux were part of the Magdalenian culture.

millennia: Thousands of years. A **millennium** is a period of one thousand years.

mythical: Existing in stories handed down over many generations from one generation to the next.

Neanderthal: A species of human, *Homo neanderthalensis,* that lived in Europe, the Middle East, and central Asia from 230,000 to 30,000 years ago. Neanderthals had strong, heavy bones and a bony ridge above their eyes.

shaman: A holy person in a tribal society. Shamans can be both healers and people who are able to communicate with the spirit world.

totem: An animal or other natural object that has a special relationship to a tribe or clan.

unicorn: A mythical horselike animal with one horn in the middle of its forehead.

For Further Reading

Allman, William F. "The Dawn of Creativity." *U.S. News & World Report,* May 20, 1996, pp. 53–58.

Bower, Bruce. "Visions on the Rocks." *Science News,* October 5, 1996, pp. 216–17.

Gould, Stephen Jay. "Up against a Wall." *Natural History,* July 1996, pp. 16–22.

Leroi-Gourhan, André. *The Hunters of Prehistory.* New York: Atheneum, 1989.

Rigaud, Jean-Philippe. "Art Treasures from the Ice Age: Lascaux Cave." *National Geographic,* October 1988, pp. 482–99.

Bibliography

Allman, William F. "The Dawn of Creativity." *U.S. News & World Report,* May 20, 1996, pp. 53–58.

Bataille, Georges. *Lascaux: La Peinture Préhistorique ou la Naissance de l'Art.* Geneva: Editions d'Art Albers Skira, 1994.

Bower, Bruce. "Visions on the Rocks." *Science News,* October 5, 1996, pp. 216–17.

Cahuvet, Jean-Marie, Éliette Brunel Deschamps, and Christian Hillaire. *Dawn of Art: The Chauvet Cave.* New York: Harry N. Abrams, 1995.

Delluc, Brigitte, Gilles Delluc, and Ray Delvert. *Discovering Lascaux.* Paris: Sud Quest, 1990.

"German Mine Yields Ancient Hunting Spears." *Science News,* March 1, 1997, p. 134.

Gore, Rick. "The Dawn of Humans: The First Europeans." *National Geographic,* July 1997, pp. 96–113.

Gould, Stephen Jay. "Up against a Wall." *Natural History,* July 1996, pp. 16–22.

Leroi-Gourhan, André. *The Hunters of Prehistory.* New York: Atheneum, 1989.

Mithen, Steven. *The Prehistory of the Mind.* London: Thames and Hudson, 1996.

Rigaud, Jean-Philippe. "Art Treasures from the Ice Age: Lascaux Cave." *National Geographic,* October 1988, pp. 482–99.

Scarre, Chris. *Smithsonian Timelines of the Ancient World.* New York: Dorling Kindersley, 1993.

"Spanish Fossils Enter Human Ancestry Fray." *Science News,* May 31, 1997, p. 333.

Vouv, J., J. Brunet, P. Vidal, and J. Marsal. *Lascaux en Périgord Noir.* Périgueux, France: Fanlac, 1992.

Index

Page numbers for illustrations are in bold face

About the Author

Dorothy Patent is the author of more than one hundred science and nature books for children and has won numerous awards for her writing. She has a Ph.D. in zoology from the University of California, Berkeley.

Although trained as a biologist, Dorothy has always been fascinated by the human past. At home, next to the books about animals, her shelves are jammed with titles such as *Mysteries of the Past.* When the opportunity came to write about other times and cultures for children, Dorothy plunged enthusiastically into the project. In the process of researching the FROZEN IN TIME series, she said, "I have had some great adventures and have come to understand much more deeply what it means to be human."

Dorothy lives in Missoula, Montana, with her husband, Greg, and their two dogs, Elsa and Ninja. They enjoy living close to nature in their home at the edge of a forest.